AMON!
THE ULTIMATE TEXAN

The theatrical production of *AMON! The Ultimate Texan* had its world premiere on May 9, 2019, at Artisan Center Theater in Hurst, Texas.

Artisan Center Theater's mission is to enrich the community with high-quality, family-friendly entertainment that warms the heart, uplifts the spirit, and tells worthy stories; to provide volunteer opportunities; and to offer ongoing education and experience in the performing arts.

artisanct.com • 817-284-1200
444 E. Pipeline Road, Hurst, Texas 76053

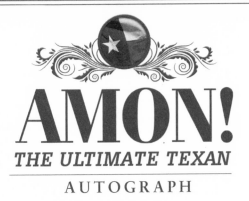

AMON!
THE ULTIMATE TEXAN
AUTOGRAPH

To Tracy—
Dave Lieber

AMON! The Ultimate Texan
Copyright © 2019 by Yankee Cowboy Publishing
First Edition, May 2019
Second Printing, September 2019

ISBN 978-0-9836149-1-3 (Hardcover)
ISBN 978-0-9836149-2-0 (Audiobook)
Library of Congress Control Number: 2019902306

Yankee Cowboy Publishing
P.O. Box 123
Keller, TX 76244-0123
(800) 557-8166
Email: publisher@yankeecowboy.com

Author website: DaveLieber.org
Play website: AmonPlay.com

This is the companion book to the theatrical production
AMON! The Ultimate Texan, which had its world stage debut on
May 9, 2019, at Artisan Center Theater in Hurst, Texas.

Cover by Tamara Dever; Interior by Monica Thomas
TLC Book Design, TLCbookdesign.com

Printed in Canada.

YANKEE
COWBOY
PUBLISHING

AMON!

THE ULTIMATE TEXAN

DAVE LIEBER

Also by Dave Lieber

The Dog of My Nightmares:
Stories by Texas Columnist Dave Lieber

Dave Lieber's Watchdog Nation:
Bite Back When Businesses and
Scammers Do You Wrong

Bad Dad

The High-Impact Writer:
Ideas, Tips & Strategies to Turn Your
Writing World Upside Down

The Best of The Black Cow:
Great Writing by Great Kids

I Knew Rufe Snow Before He Was a Road
(with Tim Bedison)

Give Us a Big Hug
(with Tim Bedison)

Shop at DaveLieber.org

This book is dedicated to my wife,
Karen Lieber,
an enthusiastic partner in
my many adventures.

This book is also dedicated to the thousands of
past employees of the *Fort Worth Star-Telegram*,
who gave a century of service to their community
of Fort Worth, Texas. Where the West begins.

Contents

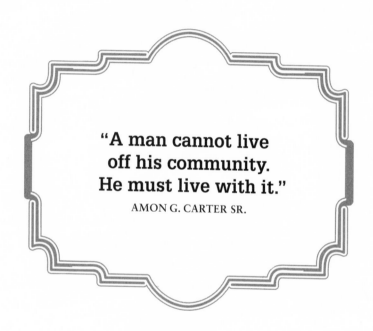

"A man cannot live
off his community.
He must live with it."

AMON G. CARTER SR.

Foreword

By DAVE LIEBER

M Y INTEREST IN THE LIFE of Amon G. Carter began my
first week at his newspaper, in 1993. He died 38 years
before, but as I would come to see, it was still his paper.

I was hired for my dream job as a metro columnist, but
that first week my new bosses assigned me to serve on the
Fort Worth Star-Telegram picnic committee.

The picnic committee? Really? In my prior job as a reporter
at *The Philadelphia Inquirer* I wrote about the Mafia! None
of the five newspapers I previously worked at ever held a staff
picnic.

At the first meeting, we were given bright yellow T-shirts
that boasted we were members of the official 1993 picnic
committee.

What's going on here?

Turns out that Amon, as publisher, had begun this company
tradition decades before—along with Christmas bonuses,
half-priced season tickets for staffers to Texas Christian University football games and, most important, generous checks
to hundreds of local charities and the newspaper's pet causes.

This was all new to me. The *Star-Telegram* was surely a
different kind of newspaper.

Even though Amon died almost four decades before I arrived in Texas, his spirit hovered at the newspaper. I began to feel his ghostly presence. The S-T did things that no other paper I knew of did. One example: The paper gave millions of dollars to community groups, not just in free advertising but in cold hard cash. And the reason was Amon. He believed a newspaper was supposed to report the news, but he also believed newspapers had a strong obligation to build their communities, too.

The more I learned about Amon, and the longer I worked at the S-T, I began to understand that his traditions and sensibilities were so strong that even decades later and under new corporate ownership, the paper still behaved in a way that would have made Amon proud.

Amon Carter Sr., at the microphone, treating employees to an annual company picnic. Long after he was gone, that Carter tradition—one of many—continued.

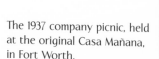

The 1937 company picnic, held at the original Casa Mañana, in Fort Worth.

He was long gone, but his office remained a semi-shrine. His 38-foot Chris-Craft boat, known as *"The Star-Telegram Yacht,"* still docked at Eagle Mountain Lake. (I once rode on it at—what else—a company picnic.) Even the annual company awards were called "Amons." Winners received a foot-tall statue of Amon holding out his famed Shady Oak hat as a gift.

Even though I won national writing awards for my work, I never won an Amon. It still bugs me that I don't have one of those cute statues. Why not? Maybe because I was somewhat of a misfit for the paper, but that turned out to be more of a strength than a weakness. As someone who grew up on the Upper West Side of Manhattan, I saw things as an outsider. I wrote three columns a week for readers who were mostly conservative, Baptist, Republican, married, native Texans. Last thing many of these good folks wanted in their beloved S-T was a columnist who was a liberal, divorced, Democratic, New York City Jew. I doubt Amon would have hired me.

After a few years of grief from my readers about my background, I decided to make fun of it. I created a cartoonish character called J.R. Lieber, the Yankee Cowboy Everybody Loves to Hate. He wore a leopard-skin jacket and a crunched-up cowboy hat that was more appropriate for *The Beverly Hillbillies* than a Texas cowboy.

The Yankee Cowboy could write things that Dave Lieber couldn't. I made J.R. president of a civil rights organization called YANKS, which stood for You Are Not Kind Southerners. I wrote columns in his voice, performed as him and, in 2000, ran him for vice president of the United States. Vote Bush-Yankee Cowboy!

This quasi-comic activity attracted the attention of legendary Texas writer Jerry Flemmons. A S-T writer and columnist, he wrote a book called *Amon: The Texan Who Played Cowboy for America*. Flemmons makes the case that Amon is the one who created the American archetype of the Western cowboy. Amon dressed up in garish cowboy garb, sometimes carried a six-shooter and loved to whoop it up and holler. In his prime, Amon was America's best-known cowboy, even though he was more businessman than ranch hand. It was all a show to promote Texas.

After I read the book and learned the immensity of Amon's life, I talked to Flemmons. Told him how much I loved his biography. Shared with him the faraway dream I had of turning Amon's life into a one-man play. I had never written a play before, but Amon's life story cried out for such a treatment.

Jerry laughed and told me with certainty that such a play would never be performed because Amon's family members were not fans of his work. Twenty years later, thanks to Artisan Center Theater in Hurst, Texas, which premiered the play, his prophecy proved wrong.

Unfortunately, Jerry is no longer with us. But I do have his autograph in my copy of his book: "With admiration to my friend and columnist colleague, Dave Lieber. If you're going to play cowboy, you may as well learn from the master—and discover the glories of his historic newspaper."

Amon was a master of so much. Of building relationships. Of extracting money for all manner of causes from every business in town. Of never accepting no for an answer. He was a master marketer. One of the best this country has ever known. His newspaper was the largest in Texas. And most important, he made things happen. Schools. Roads. State parks. So many charitable endeavors.

Four years after I arrived at his paper, I knew that I wanted to follow his philosophy of being part of the community and working to make it better. With the complete support of the *Star-Telegram*, I started a charity called SummerSanta.org, which in its first 20 years has raised more than a million dollars and sent thousands of area children to summer camps. Summer Santa provides toys to charities for summertime distribution, shares books, and pays for back-to-school clothing and athletic league scholarships. Summer Santa is all volunteer with zero paid staff and no physical office. Money raised goes directly to our children's programs.

For this, I won the Will Rogers Humanitarian Award from the National Society of Newspaper Columnists as the U.S. columnist who did the most to help his community. The award consisted of a smaller version of the famous statue of Rogers that resides in the U.S. Capitol. Will Rogers was Amon's best friend. If I had ever won that Amon statue, the two could still be together on my shelf.

The S-T played a deep role in my personal life, too. In October of 1994, I wrote the most important column of my life—a public marriage proposal to Karen, her two children and their crazy dog. "Here in Texas, I've met the woman of my dreams," it begins. "Unfortunately, she lives with the dog of my nightmares." It ended with the magic words, "Karen, will you marry me?"

She said yes, and a new world opened for me and for my readers. With my new family, I wasn't such a misfit anymore. Texas embraced me, or did as much as it could for any dude who grew up in Manhattan.

Twenty years after I arrived at the paper, I got laid off. It wasn't personal. Over time, almost everyone at the paper lost their job.

I wasn't bitter. Rather, I was grateful that I got to work and play as a newspaper columnist at a paper that let me spread my wings.

The *Dallas Morning News* scooped me up, and I continued to write my popular "Watchdog" investigative column there. After all those years at the S-T, where I was taught to write Fort Worth/Dallas and not the other way around, suddenly I was a leading member of the enemy paper in the enemy town. It felt strange.

As the 500-year-old newspaper industry comes crashing down, the time has come to tackle this project and bring Amon G. Carter back to life. Newspapers have the power to change the world. Amon understood that better than anyone. William Randolph Hearst used his media empire to make money. Amon used it to make Fort Worth and West Texas a better place to live and work. He also made a lot of money.

Picture me sitting at my keyboard as I write this, wearing my Amon Carter Shady Oak hat (I bought one at Peters Brothers in downtown Fort Worth). That's the same hat Amon gave to Babe Ruth, Franklin Delano Roosevelt and many other stars of the first half of the 20th century.

In his hat, I hear his voice. I hope while reading this book, you hear it, too.

This book and its companion play is my love letter to newspapers, to journalism, to the thousands of people who worked at the S-T during its century of glory. But mostly, it's a love letter to wonderful Fort Worth, Texas. Where the West begins. And where my dreams came true.

DAVE LIEBER
"The Yankee Cowboy"
May 2019

ENTER AMON'S WORLD!

Fort Worth Texas

Written by Cindy Walker
Sung by Ray Price

They sing songs about Chicago all the time
San Francisco and New York, they're all fine!
But there's a song that's written on this heart of mine
About a town, the best around! Let me tell ya!

Fort Worth, No words could tell its worth
Fort Worth, Texas, Best town on earth.
It's Up Town and it's Down Town and it's Cowtown too.
And there's no where like people there say,
Howdy Doo, Glad to see you
Fort Worth, Texas is western swing,
it's Van Cliburn and fiddle strings
It's everything I want and when I want to settle down
Fort Worth, Texas, That's my town.
Fort Worth, Texas, That's my town!

Fort Worth, Texas is ridin' broncs
Warm hearts, cold beer and honky tonks.
It's cowboy tales, the Chisholm Trail and memories
Bob Wills Music and Bill Mack and Symphonies
Let me tell ya!
Fort Worth, Texas is Bar-B-Que, Amon Carter and T.C.U.
It's great and let me state, there ain't no other place around
Like Fort Worth, Texas, That's my town.
Fort Worth, Texas, That's my town!

Meet
Amon Carter

WELL, HELLO EVERYONE. Or howdy strangers, as we like to say in West Texas. I'm Amon G. Carter Sr. Some people say the G stands for Gosh Darn, or something like that.

Welcome to my newspaper. The *Fort Worth Star-Telegram*. We distribute to the entire nation of Texas. We are—or were when I ran things in the first half of the 20th century—the largest newspaper in Texas.

We serve 350,000 square miles—the size of New England—every day with a newspaper. We go as far as 700 miles west of Fort Worth. We even drop bundles out of an airplane every morning to hit the good folks of West By God Texas. I am the founder, the publisher, the chief promoter of all things Fort Worth, not Dallas. To be clear. NOT DALLAS!

In my lifetime, 1879–1955, I do believe I brought a trillion dollars worth of business to Fort Worth, Texas. And I'll show you how I did it.

Early *Star-Telegram* building in downtown Fort Worth (circa 1913).

Hooray for Texas

I served as Texas' No. 1 press agent. I dressed as a cowboy. I raised heck like a cowboy. And I pushed Texas to the forefront of American life like no other person. People thought of Texas, they thought of Amon G. Carter.

People are sometimes embarrassed by my enthusiasm. I can't help myself. I love Texas so much, I want to tell the world.

I once rode a stage coach on Wall Street in Manhattan. When I visit the president at the White House, I like to stay at the Mayflower Hotel. Hotel staff is never surprised by anything I do.

I like to stand on my chair in the hotel restaurant and announce my presence with my favorite cheer: HOOOOOOOOORAAAAAAY FOR FORT WORTH AND... WEST TEXAAAASSSSSS!

Notice I don't mention Dallas.

In My Office

I've had a lot of secretaries, but only one lasted forever.
Katrine Deakins. She puts up with me, protects me and even
copes with my mad spells. God love you, Katrine.

Speaking of Katrine, I wonder where today's papers are.

"Katrine, you got my papers?"

Oh, here she comes.

*"No, I'm not mad, girl. Just a little impatient. I got a big
sales meeting here. I gotta meet all these readers looking at
this book I'm writing."*

And I do like you, folks. Yes, I do. In fact, I'm gonna put
each of you down to buy a full-page ad. You think I'm kid-
ding? Welcome to Amon Carter's Full-Page Ad Club. Where
nobody says no to me because I'm Amon Gosh Darn Carter!

That'll be $87.50, but don't worry, you have 30 days to
pay me. And I DO appreciate ya!

Shady Oak Hat

If we're gonna be spending a little bit of time together and
since you're now my newest advertiser, I want to tell you
about my hat. Its style is called Shady Oak, named after my
weekend retreat and chief party house at Lake Worth. The
hats are made special for me and my friends. I get 'em at
Peters Brothers in downtown Fort Worth.

I give them away, to football teams that win, to presidents—
Franklin D. Roosevelt has two!—to friends and celebrities
like Will Rogers, my gosh darn poker-playing pal. And once
I gave away two thousand to every delegate at the American
Petroleum Institute convention here in Fort Worth.

They cost $40 each. You can wear them in Washington or
New York, and all my friends do. See, I want the message of
Fort Worth, that we're the best little city in the world, to go

Amon in his *Star-Telegram* office in 1949. Decades after his death the office remained a semi-shrine. Recently, Bob Simpson, an oil and gas executive, owner of the Texas Rangers and ardent historical preservationist, restored the building and Amon's office to its original state.

Amon was one of America's best-known cowboys because that's the image he wanted the world to see. Here, he posed at his Shady Oak Farm, his weekend retreat where he hosted many of his parties.

beyond our borders. Inside, each hat says "Shady Oak Farm, Fort Worth, Texas. Where the West begins."

You see, a good hat represents the strength and sturdiness of West Texas. The hat is a gift all men like. It's a symbol of one's loyalties. When I give you one of my hats, it's like you are part of the Texas knighthood. You see? Good. Gosh darn it. I knew you would.

Check out the hats. Members of the White House press corps posed in their new Shady Oak hats during a 1936 visit to Amon's Shady Oak Farm.

Gifts to the President

"Katrine, come in and take a letter, please."

To Franklin D. Roosevelt
The White House, Washington, D.C.

Dear Mr. President, I am sending you by prepaid express the special hat made especially for the president. It is supposed to be the finest hat ever made.

It is the same style you have worn in the past. I hope it will fit. This hat is insured for a year for $150 and the pre-paid policy is enclosed. In addition, this hat is guaranteed for life.

I've had a plate placed in the hat box—"Franklin D. Roosevelt, Washington, D.C."—as I figure this will be your permanent address from now on. Mr. President, please, also, have your assistant send me the hat sizes of each of your top executive staff.

I will be sharing some Texas gifts during your next visit through our beloved town. May the season bring you, Mrs. Roosevelt and all of your family continued good health and happiness. May you live long and continue your great work on behalf of humanity.

Most sincerely, Amon G. Carter

"Got that? OK, wait. Katrine, one more thing."

P.S. I am forwarding to you some Shady Oak Top Crop pecans, pickled onions and Texas pink grapefruit. Enjoy!

The exquisite hat that Amon gave President Franklin D. Roosevelt
as a Christmas gift in 1941. The hat came with a lifetime guarantee.

Amon's Time Machine

FOR THE PURPOSES of me sharing this story with you, I've created a time machine. Here's how this works.

The Shady Oak hat is our time machine. I can tell it a year, snap my fingers 👆, and we'll all go there. Backward or forward. Watch this. Here we go.

1922, please. 👆

Look. I am starting one of the first radio stations in America. WBAP. We Bring A Program. So old that it doesn't begin with the letter "K" like most stations in the West. Isn't this something?

Words and songs through the air. So different than a newspaper. It cost me $300 to get it going. If this is going to be a menace to newspapers, we had better own the menace.

We're starting at 10 watts of power. Not much. But in a few years, we'll be a 50,000-watt powerhouse, and people will hear us across the U.S. Well, those with these here radios at least.

And they'll get to hear me and also local singing groups, church choirs and neighborhood bands.

Oh, hear that cowbell? That's the signal we use to let everyone know their favorite show is on. Everybody loves the bell.

First Texas Television

OK, let's all go to another year.

1948.

Katrine is wheeling in my first television. Look how big! It's radio with pictures. In 1948 I started WBAP-TV on the television. The first television station south of St. Louis, east of Los Angeles and west of Richmond, Virginia. It's our first broadcast.

I got one camera down by the rail station, and look! There's President Harry Truman visiting Fort Worth. Our first show. And it's happening there, right now, in that box.

It's magic.

Only thing is, I don't see how I can make any money off this. It's a toy, but I don't see it making anyone rich. I mean, at first, we only go on the air four hours a night from Wednesday through Sunday. Hardly anyone in Fort Worth even has one of these.

But that changes. A few years hence, in 1954, I put on the first color television show here and…

Gosh darn it. Truman ain't wearing my hat that I gave him. Aw, that's just swell. People are going to notice.

That little bum from Missouri! He ain't no FDR. He couldn't wear my hat because his stupid head is too small!

I'm so sorry. I have what Katrine calls my mad spells when things don't go my way. See, I care about the details. If he

Notice the television truck in the middle of the crowd at a 1948
campaign visit to Fort Worth by President Harry Truman.
This was the first TV broadcast in Texas.

Amon, left, and President Truman, discussed hats. U.S. House Speaker
Sam Rayburn is at right. Amon was probably showing the president how
the inside label of his hat reads, "Fort Worth. Where the West begins."

don't wear my hat, that means Fort Worth loses some of its shine. It means West Texas don't get the respect she deserves. Him not wearing that hat is like a...a...declaration of war against Amon Carter. And by God a war against Amon Carter is a war against Texas. Yes, that's right.

HOOOOOOOOORAAAAAY FOR FORT WORTH AND... WEST TEXAAAASSSSSS!

In a rare public appearance without his signature hat, Amon addressed a small audience of viewers and introduced them to television, 1948.

RCA Chairman David Sarnoff, left, in his new Shady Oak hat, visited
Fort Worth in 1954 to help Amon inaugurate the first color broadcasts in
the Southwest. Television executives bragged to the public that they
were now offering shows in "living color."

WBAP-TV a Success

Oh, we figured out how to make money off that TV. Commercials!!! Yes, commercials. I love me some commercials!

Let's see, in the very first month we sold ads to Leonard
Brothers Department Store to sponsor twenty high school
football games at $500 a pop for $10,000. We sold to Humble
Oil, Bulova, Chesterfield cigarettes and Burlington-Rock
Island Railroad. We made $47,878 in ad money right out of
the gate with this here television.

My Media Empire

They call my properties a media empire. My newspaper
prints 13 different editions every day and night. We've got a

network of 600 correspondents helping us across the state. Amon's Army is everywhere.

We cover some 1,100 towns. My boys are like celebrities. When legendary ranch editor Frank Reeves shows up in a town, every farmer and rancher for 500 miles in all directions knows who he is. Flem Hall is a more famous sports writer than Damon Runyon. When Silliman Evans went to Pampa for a story, they threw him an appreciation dinner.

You should see what they do for me!

Amon's Origin Story

W HAT'S KINDA FUNNY about this is when I was born, I
was born into nothing. I started working as a child. Had
to. And I sold things. Sold things to people they didn't know
they wanted.

The whole newspaper thing began over some cow manure.
Actually kind of a legendary story.

I met a man who told me he could create fuel by combining
crude oil with cow manure. So I went down to see this at the
Fort Worth Stockyards—and it didn't work. No. Not at all.
It stunk like a skunk backed up in the corner.

But I met a coupla fellows there, and we got to talking. And
next thing you know I'm their advertising sales manager for
the *Fort Worth Star* newspaper. And eventually, we bought
the *Telegram*, and oh, you can figure the rest.

Before he became publisher, Amon was the newspaper's business manager.
This is his early office. You can tell how early because the sign
on the wall says the circulation is 20,000 newspapers a day.
Amon would multiply that many times over.

At first, I didn't know newspapers from pecans. But I knew one thing. I knew how to sell. Sell, sell, sell. Look at you. You're a member of Amon's Full-Page Ad Club, gosh darn it.

Here's my secret. To do business with someone, you must first win their confidence. It is not what you say that impresses them, but how you say it. Never get discouraged. Do not expect to sell to everybody, OK? End of lesson.

Prepping Junior

I was teaching that lesson to little Amon Jr. the other day.

That little boy. My little Cowboy. I am leaving that boy quite a legacy when I retire. I haven't told you about my family, have I?

Well, I got a wife, or wives, if you count. Three in all. No, no. Not at the same time. And I got kids. Amon Jr., Bertice and Ruth. Ruth is the smart one. But don't be like her mother and ask me why Ruth can't run the media empire. She could, but she's a girl and that has never happened.

I'm sorry Ruth, my Sugar Pie!

Christmas Day 1939. Stylish in their vicuna coats are, from left, Amon Jr., Ruth, Dad and Nenetta, Amon's second wife and the mother of Amon Jr. and Ruth.

Promoting Fort Worth

I drill for oil—and until recently always missed. But one day I hit it big. When I sell my holdings, my sales price was said to be the biggest oil deal ever.

My kids will never want for anything for the rest of their lives. But money aside, my job is to promote Fort Worth.

That's what Amon Carter does. Amon Carter promotes Fort Worth.

We are the best city. And sometimes for the attention, I do admit that I make a little scene. I like to dress up and play cowboy. It's what the Easterners expect of us, so I will, in fact, give them a big show.

I love to play.

"Now riding a bull is Amon Gosh Darn Carter!"

"Yippeeeee! Whoopee! Hoooooo-e-e-e-e! Round 'em up. Head 'em off little dogie yonder! Yippee-yi-yo-ki-yay!"

Playing cowboy at Shady Oak Farm. See that big "Howdy Stranger" sign above him? It had been the centerpiece of the 1936 Frontier Centennial.

Always the center of attention, Amon led the
TCU band in a pep rally at the 1939 Sugar Bowl.

Amon's Shady Oak Farm was party central. The bar was big enough,
for sure. Always well-stocked, even during Prohibition.

When executives from companies doing business in Fort Worth came to town, Amon invited them to a party and insisted they sit atop his horse for a souvenir photo. Something to remember Texas by.

The Sack
Lunch Story

I F ANYONE KNOWS anything about me, it's my rivalry with
Dallas. You probably heard I'm not too popular in Dallas.
But Dallas is not too popular with me.

Dallas is my competition in everything. Nothing I like
more than beating those stuffed-shirt jerks over on the other
side of our local airport—what they call Amon Carter Field.
My friend, Jack Garner, he was vice president of these United
States, put it this way:

"Amon wants the government of the United States to run
for the exclusive benefit of Fort Worth and, if possible, to the
detriment of Dallas."

Yep, that's right. That's who I am. Amon Carter, lover of
Fort Worth and Weeessssst Texas. But not Dallas.

I don't take ads from Stanley Marcus because his store
Neiman Marcus, or as I like to call it, Needless Markups, is
in Dallas. Open one here Mr. Stanley, and then we can talk!

I buy everything I need in Fort Worth. And you should, too.

I suppose you heard the story of the sack lunch. It's not true, not necessarily, but it's the one story that if anyone knows anything about me at all, they know it. It's said that when I have to go to Dallas and meet those tin-horned bankers, I carry my own sack lunch because I don't want to spend a dime in Dallas.

Is it true? Well...it all depends on how hungry I am.

I do carry a can of gas in my car because I won't go to a Dallas filling station. I won't go to a barbershop there for a shave. Fort Worth gets my petty cash.

As I told Damon Runyon, the second-best sportswriter, my Fort Worth and Dallas have tried to bury the hatchet many times. But somebody always leaves the handle sticking out.

Know this: Fort Worth is where the West begins and Dallas is where the East peters out. Got that? Or this one:

Bring in the liquor,
On with the mirth.
To hell with Dallas,
Boost Fort Worth.

Heck, I'll drink to that.

To you, my new advertiser. Without you, I'd have a hole in my profit sack.

Shots Fired

I DIDN'T MAKE A LOT OF MISTAKES IN LIFE. Quite the contrary. But I do carry regrets about the 1928 Democratic convention.

I'll tell you about those shots I supposedly fired from the hotel in Houston. Is it true or not? My family and the newspaper editors always defended me, but, well, actually, uh, there were two times it happened. Same day, too.

Time travelers, let's go.

1928. 👏
Here we are in Houston at the Rice Hotel for the first Democratic convention in the South since before the Civil War. Time for us Texans to shine. Cactus Jack Garner is my guy for president.

Now my Rotary Club, knowing my penchant for giggle water, made me take a vow of sobriety.

"I, Amon Gosh Darn Carter, may not partake of the silly juice at this here political convention. So help me God."

Yes, yes, I admit it, I break my vow as a loyal Rotarian. But whoooopppeee. It's the Democratic convention, so let's all drink to that.

So on the convention's third day, we're in the lobby waiting for an elevator, and the thing keeps passing us by. I have one of Amon's mad spells, and I grab Sheriff Smith's pretty little pistol out of his holster, a six-shooter. And I shout: "You dang elevator! Get here now!" And I shoot the gun at the elevator shaft.

Pow, pow, pow, pow!

How many shots? I don't know. Four? Six? Anyway, it works. The elevator stops. Cops come but since no one's hurt, they don't care. It makes the newspapers everywhere. "CRAZED TEXAN PUBLISHER SHOOTS UP DEMO-CRATIC CONVENTION ELEVATOR." Heck, I'd even buy a paper to read THAT.

I lie about it. Had to. I tell the *Saturday Evening Post* "No shots were fired." This makes Fort Worth look bad. I can't have that.

Shots Fired Again

Then, you know, I do it again. I know. I know. But it's the giggle water. Those darn Rotarians were right on the money.

I go see the writer H.L. Mencken in his hotel room. We're pals. Or were. I'm trying to talk. He wants to write. So I don't know. I want to entertain him. So I play cowboy. I get up and for no reason fire my pistol out the hotel window. Three shots this time. You know, I never admitted this before.

I learn later that my shots hit a room across the street that the Ku Klux Klan is using for meeting space. I get a few compliments on that.

Amon liked to whip out his gun. He did it in 1938 as a startled
U.S. Assistant Secretary of War, Louis Johnson, turns away.

In this 1945 photo, he pulled out a gun at a card game at his house.

I also get to meet several Texas Rangers. I tell them a cock and bull story that Mencken did it, but please don't arrest him because he's an important guest of the great state of Texas. And they buy it.

I wish I had enough Shady Oak hats to give to all those policemen I met at that hotel. But I've invited them out west for a ride on the *Star-Telegram's* yacht.

So lesson here is if you're going to do something stupid, don't do it, as I did, in front of H.L. Mencken. He was furious—and later wrote about it in his memoirs.

In his book, he called my shooting for no reason—and I quote—"a natural sign of discontent in Texas." I call it a natural sign of the giggle water.

My Best Friend

"Katrine, how come you can't get Will Rogers on the phone? Either you're not trying hard enough or he's avoiding me. Which is it?"

Will Rogers. You heard of him, right? He's on the radio. He writes a newspaper column that's in almost every paper in America. Why, he's the most famous man in this country.

And I'm proud to say he's my best friend. The brother I never had. Oh, Will and me. We've spent plenty a night in the Fort Worth Club in my suite, 10G, playing poker. Son of a gun owes me $500 from the last game. Gosh darn.

"Katrine?! You got Will yet? OK, keep trying Owes me $500. I've got to go out. I'll check back in a few minutes."

My Early Start at Selling

Let's go.

1879.

I want to show you something. It's Dec. 11, 1879. We're in Crafton, Texas. In a log cabin built by my father. A terrible winter storm is raging.

Look! There's me being born.

I want to show you how I was born into nothing. We moved to Bowie, and as a boy all I did was work. Left school in the eighth grade. I start out as a handyman, then a chamber maid and a janitor. I get room and board in Millie Jarrott's boarding house. Plus, she pays me $1.50 a week for doing chores.

Let's see. I sell peaches, assist a doctor, work in a confectionary shop selling ice cream and candy. I make soda pop in a bottling plant. For the weekend horse races, I open a refreshment stand. I collect and resell empty whiskey bottles. I sell and sell and sell.

In 1930, Amon returned
to visit the log cabin he
was born in. Here, he
posed with boyhood
pal George Turner.

When President Franklin D. Roosevelt's train passed through Bowie in 1938,
his entourage saw this tribute to native son Amon Carter, who as a young
teen lived and worked in this 19th-century boarding house.

My biggest success is my chicken sandwich business. My pals and I are called the "chicken and bread boys."

See, the Fort Worth and Denver train stops in Bowie for water. I'd rush on board with chicken sandwiches. I get all my boys—John, Mose, Shorty, R.J. and Tan—to work the trains with me, I would buy a whole cooked chicken for 25 cents and sell each sandwich for 10 cents. I usually make two whole dollars a day.

Heck, I never forgot my roots. Long time later, when my friend Franklin Delano Roosevelt stopped in Bowie on his campaign train, I jumped on board with a basket of chicken sandwiches.

I handed Franklin a chicken sandwich and asked for 10 cents.

I said, "Thank you, sir, Mr. President."

Still have that dime. Means everything to me. From the chicken and bread boys all the way to the White House. That's my life.

When the president's train stopped in Bowie in 1938, Amon re-created his early job as a "chicken and bread boy." He even sells the president a sandwich for a dime.

For Amon, this moment when the president's train stopped in the town where he grew up showed the true power of Amon Carter, king of West Texas. He brought the president to town!

My Newsies

You know who I like best at my paper? Not my editors or reporters.

I'll tell ya—I care most for the news boys.

They fight for street corners to sell my editions.

Tough little boys, often poor, hard-working, gruff, manipulative, creative.

I look at them and see little me.

These kids know what sells. What headline. Which story. Most popular comic strip.

Over the years, some of my newsboys rise to the top of corporate America. They look back fondly on their first sales job.

Every year Amon threw a banquet in honor of his beloved corps of loyal newsboys. As part of the tradition, he gave each boy a silver dollar.

Every year, I throw a big banquet for all my boys. Tell them how special they are. Give each a silver dollar. They get Thanksgiving and Christmas gifts, too. I even set up a fund to provide for them. Love those boys.

Never Accept No

When I became advertising manager for the *Fort Worth Star* all that work taught me how to sell. I didn't take no for an answer. I sold every ad in the paper. But that wasn't enough to pay the bills.

I bought a peach orchard near Arlington, between Fort Worth and the pretend city that starts with a "D." After work I boarded a street car to the orchard, picked and packed my peaches and returned them to Fort Worth around midnight.

I'd sleep till 5 a.m., deliver the fruit, and then head out to sell that day's ads. I loved it.

When my partners and I bought the *Telegram* and merged it to create the *Fort Worth Star-Telegram*, I knew what I needed to do. Outwork, outsell and outmaneuver everybody. It was like my old chicken-sandwich runs, but only much bigger, you know?

Guess You'd Call Me a Groupie

YOU PROBABLY KNOW by now, I don't like silence. I do like to talk. I talk to everybody. From presidents to paperboys. You can't come to Fort Worth without seeing Amon Carter.

I don't mean to brag, but I have a lotta friends you probably heard of. Let's see. Dwight Eisenhower, J.C. Penney, of course Franklin. You have a word for that today. Uh, groupie. Yeah, you could say I'm a celebrity chaser.

I bring 'em to Shady Oak Farm, or Suite 10G at the club. Gary Cooper, Babe Ruth, Jimmy Durante. The Mellons, Duponts, Firestones and Rockefellers. Of course, they all get hats.

In addition to his weekend retreat at Shady Oak, Amon and
his family lived on a beautiful estate in Fort Worth.
His house was one of the biggest in town.

Bob Hope visited Fort Worth in 1949 for a luncheon. Here he signed
a guest book, with Amon Sr. and Amon Jr. looking on.

Edgar Bergen and his little sidekick, Charlie McCarthy,
were one of the hottest acts in America.

When Gary Cooper's movie *The Westerner* opened in 1940,
Amon threw him a big party at Shady Oak and
broadcast it live on radio station WBAP.

Bonnie and Clyde

Big man like me don't scare easily.

This one time, though...

You heard of Bonnie and Clyde? Outlaw couple robbed banks in the 1930s.

In 1934, they killed two state troopers near Fort Worth.

Our banner headline: "INTENSE MAN-HUNT FOR CLYDE BARROW AND HIS CIGAR-SMOKING WOMAN COMPANION, BONNIE PARKER."

A few days later, I get a letter. It's from Clyde Barrow himself. It's rambling and rough, but the intent is clear.

> Don't let your editor make another remark about Bonnie like you did the other day. They called her a cigar-smoking woman. Another remark about my underworld mate and I will end such men as you mighty quick. I know where you and your reporters live.... We'll be seeing you soon.
> Clyde Barrow

That's one reader request I personally handled. We never called Bonnie a cigar smoker again. And the police protected my family and me until Bonnie and Clyde were put to rest.

Running Hearst Out of Town

The greatest publisher of my era was William Randolph Hearst. He owned newspapers in all the big cities. I drove him nuts.

On purpose.

He saw how good I was and he kept offering me jobs for ever bigger salaries.

He told me I could run his New York City newspaper for a large salary and with a free hand.

When that didn't work, he tried to buy the *Star-Telegram*.

When that didn't work, he started a newspaper in Fort Worth to compete.

When that didn't work, I bought him out and he was gone for good.

I out-Hearsted Hearst!

Move to New York City and leave my beloved Lone Star Texas behind?

I have made many visits to New York and am always disturbed by all the pessimism and gloom coming out of New York and the East.

Just think how lucky we are to be living in America and, especially, how lucky we are to live in Texas.

'Dear Sweet Will'

EXCUSE ME, let me take this phone call.

"At last. Will, where you been? You rope-twirling, unfunny son of a gun. I've been trying to get you all day. You avoiding me because of all the poker money you owe me? Oh, still on that movie? Thought it was done. When you coming down to 10G? OK. Good, because I have a surprise for you. Later, buddy boy."

I HATE to do this. But I must.

1935.

Once when Will came to town to do a fundraiser for drought relief, he introduced me for my speech by saying, "Just say hello and SHUT UP." Everybody laughed because no one else can get away with talking to Amon Gosh Darn Carter like that.

I drove him to the airport for a flight to Alaska. I wish to God I hadn't.

That gosh darn plane crashes in Alaska. It's the worst day of my life. I lose my best friend, my brother. It's a national tragedy. Eskimos find him and wrap his body for the trip home, I meet Will's body in Seattle. I get on that plane and sit beside Will's coffin and his pilot's—Wiley Post—all the way home. Worst airplane ride of my life.

Amon and Will Rogers were best friends. Will talked about Amon on his national radio show, making Amon a famous Texan across the land.

After Will Rogers died in a plane crash, Amon kept his friend's memory front and center, ordering statues and a painting, then getting important buildings in Fort Worth named after Will. Amon in his office in 1936.

Will Rogers, with his
newspaper column and
radio show, was for a
time the most famous
man in America.

Amon stands in front of the old Worth Theater
advertising one of Will's movies, 1928.

In Memoriam

I knew what I had to do. I'm Mr. Fort Worth.

By God! I speak for Fort Worth! And for Will's memory, Fort Worth is going to lead the way. If you have all this gosh darn power, what good is it if you don't use it? I never ran for public office, because I didn't need to. That would have slowed me down.

I get, or the paper gets—what's the difference?—the new city coliseum we were building named Will Rogers Coliseum. Same for the auditorium nearby. Fort Worth donated more money to a new foundation named after Will than any other city in America.

I paid $20,000 for a life-size statue of Will on his favorite horse, Soapsuds. Put one outside the coliseum. We put another one at Texas Tech—a college which incidentally, for the record, I should note I got started. And a third is in Oklahoma.

The statues were done in '39, but I kept the coliseum one in storage for eight years until the time to unveil it was right.

Finally, in '47, I asked General Eisenhower to come in and show the world our statue. I guess those eight years in between was me grieving. Yeah, that's what it was. At the time, though, I didn't realize that. Dear sweet Will.

Please forgive me. This is so hard to talk about. Will Rogers made a lot of people laugh. But he made me cry.

"Riding Into the Sunset," sculpted by Electra Waggoner Biggs, shows Will and his favorite horse, Soapsuds. It still rides today outside the Will Rogers Coliseum in Fort Worth.

Two new buildings named for Will Rogers in time for the opening of the 1936 Frontier Centennial were the Will Rogers Coliseum and the adjoining Will Rogers Municipal Auditorium.

Amon visited Will Rogers's grave in California. Amon was lead fundraiser for a foundation named for Will. Even Amon's beloved newsies chipped in and donated $240.

Amon wanted a life-sized tribute statue of Will Rogers placed in front of the coliseum. He paid $20,000 in 1939 for one but kept it in storage for eight years. He wanted a top-level dignitary to come and unveil it.

Finally, in 1947, Amon lands an all-star crew for the unveiling. Margaret Truman, the president's daughter, sang. General Dwight D. Eisenhower christened the statue. Here, Amon's friends and family toast the general at Amon's home. Amon's third wife, Minnie Meacham Carter, stands over Ike's left shoulder. Amon Jr. is at far right and Amon Sr. is left.

Amon arranged for a larger-than-life painting of Will to be placed inside the Will Rogers complex in Fort Worth's Cultural District. Amon made sure that Fort Worth would never forget Will Rogers.

No Fear

WILL'S DEATH HURT ME, hurt us, bad. But it didn't diminish my love of flying. Let me tell you something. My love of flying gave birth to a trillion dollars in business for my adopted hometown. I believe I can prove it to you.

It all started in 1911 when the *Star-Telegram* helped promote the arrival of daredevil pilots, the first visit by an airplane to our town. My first flight was in 1915, and I was hooked. I became an investor in a company that later became American Airlines. In fact, I maneuvered it so the company moved its headquarters from Dallas to Fort Worth. A Dallas paper wrote this headline: "Amon Cartered Again."

So, if you're counting, that's how I start figuring the trillion.

For World War I, I was among those who convinced the Army to set up three pilot training fields.

I knew all the great pilots. Charles Lindbergh, Amelia Earhart and Eddie Rickenbacker. They came by my farm for parties in their honor.

Amon, left, with Charles Lindbergh, the most famous pilot of his era.
In 1927, two years before this visit, Lucky Lindy made the first
nonstop solo flight across the Atlantic Ocean.

For World War II, I brought in the Consolidated plane factory, also known as General Dynamics. You still counting?

I got us Carswell Air Force Base.

In the 1950s, we grabbed Bell Helicopter. Now Bell's national headquarters is along the Fort Worth-Hurst border. Bell alone has built more than 35,000 aircraft. Getting closer to that trillion.

We needed a big airport in Fort Worth. People were driving to Dallas. In the 1930s I supported a joint airport midway between the cities. The terminal's front faced Fort Worth. That meant its rear faced Dallas. Dallas didn't like that. They pulled out of the deal. Said they couldn't trust me.

Amon Carter's Fort Worth airport, designed to keep locals from
driving to Dallas for an airport, only lasted 15 years.

I almost won that one. I built my own airport in Fort
Worth. Greater Southwest International Airport, also called
Amon Carter Field. Dallas tried to stop it, going all the way
to the U.S. Supreme Court. But they lost. Ha ha.

My airport opened in '53—same year as my heart attacks.
Maybe that was an omen. My airport never made it. But
my original dream did. You ever been to Dallas/Fort Worth
International Airport? Only they got the order of the two
cities wrong.

Throw in modern Fort Worth Alliance Airport, the first
industrial airport of its type, and you can see that Fort Worth's
love of and investment in flying continues to this day.

Dedication day in 1953 for Amon Carter Field, also known as
Greater Southwest International Airport. Amon couldn't attend because
he was recovering from a heart attack. His son, Amon Jr., filled in for him.

One-Person Economic Development

These days, cities have economic development departments
to attract business. Fort Worth's department was right here
in my head. Forget the mayor, whoever he is. By God, I speak
for Fort Worth!

Sometimes it was a lot simpler than it sounds. One time I
was in the New York office of Sinclair Oil when I saw a map
on the wall with a pin on Dallas representing a subsidiary. I
walked over and moved the pin to Fort Worth. It worked.
The company moved its regional office.

It's a Wonderful Life

Sometimes I couldn't move the pin. The Depression and World War II were downright scary. Tough times seemed like the natural order of things.

Do you remember the movie *It's a Wonderful Life?* Well, long before the movie that kinda happened here. The bank panic of 1930.

For some reason, and I still don't know why, people started bottling up in the lobby of First National Bank one day, demanding withdrawals. Spilled out into the street. It was a mob. A stampede! I got the call. I was home in bed with the flu.

I couldn't believe this thing when I first heard it. This is the safest bank in the world. Heck, I know cause my money's in there.

So I got dressed and drove downtown. I remember walking in the lobby. Oh, heck. Let's go there.

1930. ✋
"Excuse me, everyone! Coming through."
I make a speech:

"My good friends, this bank is as solid as any national bank can be. Let's not be deterred by rumors spread by idle gossips, busybodies and talkers. This is the safest bank in the world, as you'll soon find out.

"For every dollar it is paying you, it is taking in six more. Why right now, two million five hundred thousand dollars is coming from the Federal Reserve Bank in Dallas."

At that moment, as if on cue, armed guards sweep into the lobby carrying money bags.

"See there?! What did I tell you? You can't take your money out as fast as they can bring it in. Let's boost our city.

Let's not go mad like this. Let's go home, and in the morning your money will be right here for you. The organization I represent has a hundred thousand dollars here, and I expect to leave it here."

Lots of folks go home, but many stay. So I buy 'em all dinner. Send out for cheese sandwiches and hot dogs for everybody. Then I hire a couple of bands from the Hotel Texas to turn it into a party. They play *Singing in the Rain* and *Hail, Hail, the Gang's All Here*. Couples dance. Others sing. We pass around a jug of giggle juice.

"Hello everybody. I have an announcement to make. All you depositors can now take your bank passbooks over to the Majestic Theater for free admission to see the new all-talking picture show Officer O'Brien. *I know. You gotta love Fort Worth. Now get on out of here!"*

Winston Churchill's Hat

I get such joy giving my hats away. Usually, I give to Americans. But I had a chance to get one into the hands of British Prime Minister Winston Churchill during World War II.

I first met Churchill in London and showed him a photo of a Stetson I gave to FDR. Told him I'd be honored if he wore one.

Months later, I sent the hat to the White House and asked them to pass it on while the prime minister was visiting.

My note to Churchill stated the gift is "evidence of my appreciation of the great job you are doing."

"In Texas," I continued, "a hat is the emblem of stability and good fellowship. No one is better qualified to wear an emblem of this kind.

"With the Prime Minister of England and the President of the United States wearing a Texas hat, the country should be safe."

Churchill wrote back, "It is the most handsome hat which I shall be proud to wear, more especially for the compliment which the gift connotes."

Junior Goes
to War

YOU KNOW, aside from Fort Worth and Texas, I love my
kids. I know I'm not a great husband. A provider, yes.
But I had that suite, 10G, at the Fort Worth Club. One of my
wives, Nenetta, she once said she divorced me because she got
tired of being married to the Chamber of Commerce.

I got three kids. Little Ruth, my Sugar Pie. Bertice, who
didn't live with me. And Amon Jr.—my Cowboy. But I was
gone a lot. So I always tried to remind myself that I am a
father. I printed the children's baby pictures on *Star-Telegram*
Christmas bonus checks. In 1920, I named the new printing
presses Bertice and Amon.

When my boy was 10 years old I put him on the street
selling newspapers. By age 11, I had him up at 3 a.m. every
morning to deliver a route. Summers, he worked as a copyboy.
Then in photography and in advertising.

When he was 21, he decided he wanted to go off to war.

1942.

"Now Cowboy, you know you don't have to do this. I know everyone in the war department from A to Z—and one phone call and you're out of harm's way in an office pushing paper."

He doesn't listen to me. Cowboy is a lieutenant in the 91st Field Artillery. He told me, "I may not get back, but if I do I will have the satisfaction of feeling I have done my part."

I am so proud of him. Oh son! Bye, my Cowboy. Bye.

Like many men his age, Amon Jr. believed he had no choice but to act on his love of country and enlist to fight in World War II.

"Katrine, please send a telegram to Amon Jr."

Son, I will pay bonus for every Japanese, German and Italian soldier you kill. Keep a tab. Much love, from Dad

They send my boy to Fort Knox for training and then to North Africa, to Tunisia where Allied forces are finally circling General Rommel's army. A year later, he...wait...

In 1942 Amon Sr. visited his son in London.
The next year, Junior was captured by the Nazis.

1943. ✌

It's Valentine's Day. Also the worst day of my life. On this day, Cowboy goes missing. I got a phone call.

"Amon Carter here...Yes...My son...my...my...oh no, no, no."

I shout for Katrine.

"Katrine, we're going to have to call the generals in the war department and, of course, Franklin."

I get this war department letter telling me Cowboy is missing in action. This is a dark time. I'm crazy angry one minute, just furious and distraught the next. Oh, it's a depression.

I pray all the time now. I sometimes don't...do...anything.

Darn it. I'm Amon G. Carter and I fix things. I make the world better. I help. I give. I care. But I can't do a gosh darn thing about this. I can't find my boy. I can't rescue him. I can't be Amon Carter and fix this!

"Katrine, get me the International Red Cross in Geneva. After that I want Major General Ulio of the Army. Then I want Franklin and Eleanor."

Amon G. Carter Jr., serial number 0-402537 of the 91st Armored Field Artillery, Battery B of the First Armored Division. WHERE ARE YOU?

I receive a wonderful letter from Mrs. Roosevelt.

Dear Mr. Carter, We have just heard that your son is listed as missing and both the president and I want you to know that we realize what an anxiety this is for you. We shall hope and pray with you that you will soon have good news.
Very sincerely yours, Eleanor Roosevelt

The *Star-Telegram* covers my son's disappearance on the front page. The Texas House passes a resolution praising

Cowboy for his "Texas manhood." I vow to give up smoking cigars until my son returns.

But truth is, I've given up hope. It's been months with no word. Oh Lord, we are not going to see him again. God love his sweet soul. He certainly deserved a better fate. Still, bless his heart; it was just what he wanted to do. He would not have it otherwise.

I'm slipping. I guess it's the first time I've ever been a quitter. One thing is, it taught me how to pray, which I do every day and night.

"Lord, I can't help but believe that you and your wisdom will bring justice to all of us. So, again, I fervently ask you for this sweet youngster to have a chance and come home to his loved ones. How I wish I could take his place. Amen."

We eventually find out what happened on that terrible Valentine's Day. His commanding officer told me that he sent Junior and a sergeant out before dawn to establish a mountaintop observation post in Tunisia. German tanks moved in on the rest of the squad, and the men got retreat orders. But the son of a gun forgot to tell Junior and the sergeant. Forgot? Gosh darn. Forgot!!

For a day, my boy kept his position, then he and the sarge slipped out. They wandered for 10 days, hiding at night in caves and ravines, shivering in the cold. For food, they chewed on the insides of cactus.

They were found by the locals, who beat the daylights out of them with sticks and fists. The women spit on him. They robbed him of his camera, six-shooter, his watch, money and all his clothes and turned him over to the Germans. Amon Jr. was loaded in a cattle car with other captured officers and shipped to Poland. You'll excuse me. This is so difficult.

A few months go by. I get some news.

1944.

*"Hey everybody. I got this telegram. Oh my Lord. Amon
Jr. is alive. He's alive. Do you hear me?*

*"EVERYBODY! AMON JR. IS ALIVE. Oh, thank you
Lord. Thank you. Says here he's in Poland in a POW camp.
Prisoner of war number 1595.*

*"Katrine, tell the boys downstairs to stop the presses!
Cowboy is in a Nazi prison. Then get the war department
so I can learn about this POW camp. Wire Franklin to tell
everyone not to bomb that camp. And I need aerial photos."*

Oh, I make a lotta calls. Legend is that I even try to call
Adolf Hitler, but heck that ain't true. No speaken de Deutsch.

In letters, Amon Jr. lets us know the camp is low on food,
warm clothing and blankets. I send a truckload. We print his
letters in the *Star-Telegram*. Everyone follows it.

He was always asking for essentials. He'd ask for short
pants in the summer and warm coats in the winter. He asked
for food, for bathroom tissue, for matches. I send it all. He
wanted Dick Tracy comics, too.

Here's a favorite letter.

April 1944. Dear Dad, just received your letter of February
23. I have ordered a good wrist watch from Switzerland and
you will receive the bill in the mail. Captain Salerno, a good
friend of mine, has the same watch and it's really swell. He
got it in another camp. You don't have to wind them at all.
They wind themselves by using the motion of your arm.
Also, please send 200 cigars.
Lots of love, Amon Jr.

Sure enough. I got the bill from Switzerland. Rolex. $75.
That's my boy!

I got to thinking. We had a lot of German prisoners held in Texas. So I bought one thousand packs of cigarettes and had 'em put "Compliments of Amon Carter Jr." on the package. And we sent them to the German POWs hoping they would write home about it and Amon and his pals would get better treatment.

Another letter.

From the White House. Dear Amon, I wanted to tell you how relieved I was to know that the youngster is safely a prisoner in Germany. That is a lot better than being a prisoner in Japan. I hope to see you soon.
Always sincerely, Franklin D. Roosevelt

Cowboy was in there for two years. When the war ended in '45, I decided to go over to see him.

General Eisenhower wanted a group of newspaper publishers to travel overseas and see for ourselves what our enemies had done so the world would never forget. They called it the "Atrocities Tour."

Over in Europe we saw horrible scenes of emaciated prisoners and piles of dead bodies. I was repulsed. Sickened. But we were there to bear witness to the worst crimes the world had ever known.

After a few days of this I sneak away to find my boy.

1945.

I travel across Europe. I'm looking everywhere.

"Have you seen my son? Have you seen this boy? Have you seen Amon Carter Jr.? Have you? Have you?"

Then on May 4, we're riding in a Jeep and we meet a reporter for the *New York Herald Tribune*. When I introduce myself, he says he has a letter for me. It's from Cowboy, whom he saw earlier in the day. Amon was freed on April 22.

The American army had arrived at Junior's camp, but Russian troops refused to allow them in for a rescue. So U.S. tanks broke through the front gate and loaded the men in trucks.

We keep driving. Finally, at one stop, I hear a voice from behind say the five best words I ever heard: "Well, Dad. Here I am."

"Son! Son! Son!"

We travel around Europe for a week, and then he goes back into service.

"Bye, son. When you get home Dick Tracy and your favorite food will be waitin' on ya."

I file some front-page stories for the paper, then come home. I have a debt to pay. I had made a promise to the Lord.

"Katrine, I want you to give a thousand dollars to every church in Fort Worth…. Yes, Katrine, even the black churches. They pray, don't they? Well, gosh darn it, pay 'em."

Oh, I forgot to tell you that while I was over there, I stood on Mussolini's balcony. And guess what I did?

HOOOOOOOOORAAAAAY FOR FORT WORTH AND… WEST TEXAAAASSSSSS!

Of the thousands of photos taken of Amon during his lifetime, this was probably his favorite. It is the day in 1945 when he found his son, who had spent two years in a Nazi POW camp. The photograph ran in newspapers across America.

My Arch Rival
Dallas

YOU DO NOTICE that I leave Dallas out of that cheer? Oh, Dallas. Let me show you something.

1936. 👏

Oh, was I mad. It's the 100th birthday of Texas' independence from Mexico, but Dallas—where the East peters out—gets the Texas Centennial Exposition.

It's a big one, financed by $15 million in taxpayer money. Dallas builds onto its Fair Park. Fort Worth? We get nothing. That doesn't sit well with me.

I tell the good folks of my city, "You'd think Dallas invented Texas just because they bid higher for the Centennial than any other city. But we're going to put on a show of our own to teach those dudes where the West really begins."

I take over. I tell people to go to Dallas for education because the exhibits and buildings are about culture, but come to Fort

Worth for entertainment. I promise everyone we're going to have our own Fort Worth centennial. Only one problem: We don't have any money.

I call everyone. We run a full campaign. We get some federal money. I raid the newspaper for $65,000, which causes Bert, my money man, to have a nervous breakdown. We sell bonds for $50 each. Everybody donates. I got a strong arm. Everybody who ever got a hat hears from me.

"Thank you for your donation, sir. You'll get as many tickets as you need. I'm hiring the crew now. I'll get a thousand beautiful girls for the Frontier Follies. I'll have a Texas pageant. I'll have two thousand Indians and a thousand cowboys. The show of shows."

We call it the Frontier Centennial. We raise a million dollars. Then we have to put the show together. We build the biggest theater the Southwest had ever seen. Casa Mañana, the House of Tomorrow. A large amphitheater with a revolving stage and a lagoon. Water jets that shoot to the sky. Even has a restaurant.

I didn't do all this myself. I hired the legendary Broadway Billy Rose, the most creative man in theater. He promised to put together the greatest show ever—the *Casa Mañana Review of 1936*. I pay him a thousand buckeroos a day for 100 days.

Billy is worth it. I remember before we signed the contract, we're giving each other the once-over. This New York guy says to me, "What I'm going to lay out for you boys is pretty big."

I say, "NOTHING is too big for the state of Texas."

He says, "That's all I want to know."

We had a deal. Fort Worth stole the show. We couldn't keep 'em out.

What was it? Well, let me be frank. For this one year, one time, to beat the pants off Dallas, we in Fort Worth kinda forget our morals.

You know what did it? Nudity. Naked or near naked women. We hired the world's greatest stripper. Ever hear of Sally Rand? Greatest tease girl on the planet, only she hated that description. She was a dancer, she said. I got Broadway Billy to bring her on, and we build the Nude Ranch on site. Not the dude ranch, but the nude ranch.

Sally and her female friends would be prancing behind a screen of fans or, if there's no wind, balloons. They called it a bubble dance! She'd be naked or close to it—but outlined in a soft blue light. It was, uh, artistic! Take that Dallas!

We set it up with a sign that claimed, "The only educational exhibit on the grounds." Tickets are a quarter. I couldn't keep them away.

And inside Casa Mañana's first printed program, you have to keep flipping pages to the back, but then you'd see it. Pages of near-naked women. Forgot our morals. Make a profit. Beat Dallas.

The preachers came after us. They heard 'cause, well, I ordered hundreds of billboards spread out in nine states. Half-naked women frolicked. You couldn't see one of those billboards and not want to come.

One read: "BIGGEST ENTERPRISE DEVOTED EXCLU-SIVELY TO AMUSEMENT IN THE HISTORY OF THE WORLD."

And: "GO ELSEWHERE FOR EDUCATION, COME TO FORT WORTH FOR ENTERTAINMENT." I wrote that one.

When the preachers found out about the booze and the slot machines, they did somersaults.

We broadcast live on the radio to 85 stations across America.

You could come in and see a re-creation of Will Rogers's living room.

Ernest Hemingway was driving cross-country when he saw the billboards and stopped by.

J. Edgar Hoover came, too. I took him to the shooting gallery on the midway and beat the F.B.I. director in a rifle match. Ha! Ha! This cowboy!

I tell you what. We left Dallas in the dust. We stole all the attention. More than a million people passed through our turnstiles, walking under the welcome sign that said, Howdy Stranger.

They ate 10-cent banana splits and 15-cent ham sand-wiches, saw Sally Rand and a whole bunch of beautiful girls, cowboys and Indians. The big show ended when two bands, not one, but two, played *The Eyes of Texas*. Wasn't a dry eye in the house. Oh, my, my. Poor, poor Dallas.

Nicest letter I ever got:

> Amon, No use trying to put in words how I feel about you. If at any time I can ever be of service in any sense, write, wire, phone or whistle. As a producer, you will pardon me if I envy you. I build shows. Christ. You built a city.
> Affectionately, Billy Rose

When Amon Carter found out that Dallas had won the right to throw the state's official 100th birthday party, he erupted. He promised a bigger festival in Fort Worth and hired Broadway Billy Rose to produce the greatest theatrical production in the history of the universe.

Amon strong-armed everyone he ever gave a hat to for a donation. He made sure that a one-of-a-kind, open-air theater, a nightclub with sky called Casa Mañana, opened on time.

Broadway Billy and Amon decided that the secret to their success would be
women performers. They took it to heights never before seen in Texas.

It was more than fabulously long lines of what were called "chorus girls."

It was more than the elaborate costumes.

The big draw turned out to be nudity—or near nudity. This is the cover of the big show's program. The final pages showed photos of women with no clothes on.

At Amon's insistence, Sally Rand, the most famous "fan dancer" in the land,
was brought to town by Broadway Billy Rose, who greeted her.
She suddenly became the biggest story in Fort Worth and beyond.

With her proper hat and conservative dress, it was hard to imagine
this nice young woman making a living taking her clothes off.
Broadway Billy knew that Sally was a big draw.

Leaders of Tarrant County, where Fort Worth is county seat,
honored Sally with the "key to the county."

Sally Rand practiced with her famed balloon, but the attire
called to mind the term "full dress rehearsal."

Meanwhile, over in Dallas, at the official state birthday party, there was no Sally Rand. No Casa Mañana. But there were lots of educational exhibits. Yawn.

Amon rubbed it in. Outside Fair Park in Dallas, he arranged for this sign in lights: "Wild & Whoo-pee...Fort Worth Frontier...45 Minutes West."

Largest in the World

T HERE'S ONE OTHER TIME I went after another city like that in a big way. That darn Tulsa, Oklahoma, thing! They were getting a bomber plant built by the war department ahead of World War II. A mile-long plant manufacturing planes and what not. Think of the jobs!

We weren't getting anything. We're Fort Worth, the Queen of the Plains. Where the West begins.

I WANT the biggest bomber plant in the world. Not Tulsa.

1940.

On the phone:

"General Brett! You can't do this. We must get that new aircraft factory. Sir, with all due respect.... He hung up on me."

I call Franklin. Trust me on this. I laid the groundwork for this call going back years.

The president loves a good steak, so I always send him choice cuts from the grand champion steer at the Fort Worth Stock Show. I wrote to him:

Dear Mr. President, We are sending four choice cuts to you by American Airlines. The steaks will leave the Fort Worth Club at 7:30 a.m., depart from the airport at 8:10 and reach you in Washington at 5:41 p.m., weather permitting. It should be reposing in your ice box by 6:30 p.m. and ready for an appetizing repast.

Every year, Amon bought the grand champion steer at the
Southwestern Exposition and Fat Stock Show in Fort Worth,
held at the Will Rogers Coliseum.

Amon loved to send a live turkey to the White House.
But after several years, President Roosevelt's people told him to stop.

Likely this bird went to the White House. Amon liked to have
photographs of his most important gifts.

At Christmas, Amon sent smoked turkeys to friends and
acquaintances from coast to coast.

A gift card accompanied Amon's turkey gifts.
This one, from 1937, was addressed to FDR at the White House.

I'd send him two smoked turkeys, along with the grand champion bronze gobbler from Shady Oak Farm, alive and thoroughly prepared for Christmas activities. The old boy was 40 pounds and made for a grand White House centerpiece on Christmas Day. And I included pickles, cucumber and onion, jumbo pecans and Texas pink grapefruit.

Let's see. I sent him a special fishing lure. I recommended pork rinds on the hook. President Roosevelt kept a stamp collection, so I sometimes sent him first issues. Heck, I once even sent him a new specially made genuine Western leather belt.

Of course, I sent a lot of hats.

So when the Tulsa thing hit, and they got the bomber plant, my courtship of FDR came to the fore. All those champion beef steaks and Texas pink grapefruits were gonna have to pay off.

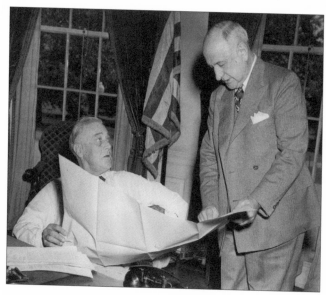

FDR and Amon, shown here in the White House, were very close. Amon liked to think of himself as FDR's "man in the Southwest." But Carter denied he had any say-so in political patronage jobs.

Amon, riding with FDR in the president's car.

Amon stood by the side of FDR's touring car as the president
cast a fishing line into Amon's stock pond. According to legend,
the president reeled in a 5-pound bass. Hmm.

Back to 1940. 👆

The federal government announces that Tulsa is getting the plant. I send a telegram:

> Dearest Franklin, No to Tulsa for aircraft plant. From your top man in the American Southwest. Fort Worth has best offer, site, climate, size and facilities.
>
> Please reconsider. It's almost a crime against national defense to permit the rejection of this site. We have no differences with Tulsa. They are a swell crowd of folks. May we have your friendly cooperation?
> Amon

"Katrine, please send out alerts by telegram to all the senators and congressmen on our list. And on those, sign Governor O'Daniel's name, not mine. He won't mind. And of course, start with our friend House Speaker Rayburn."

The darndest thing happened. We had 13 days to fix this. The Tulsa people, swell as they are, didn't know what hit 'em. They didn't send champion beef steaks to the White House. But 13 days after we threw Washington into a tizzy, we Texans won. The war department announced they were going to build two plants, each a mile long, one in Tulsa and one in Fort Worth.

"Katrine, telegram please to Franklin:"

> Franklin, bless your heart. Thanks for your timely and friendly help for which our entire citizenship is grateful.
> Amon.

When we did the groundbreaking a brigadier general said, "We're digging Hitler's grave here." I do believe that's so. We built enough great planes to win the war. And we added many thousands of new jobs. It's a mile long and 320 feet wide.

I'm happy, of course, but you know bringing that here wasn't enough. Fort Worth has to have the biggest EVERY-THING. Has to!

Phone call:

"Franklin! Hello Mr. President.

"How is Eleanor? Tell her she is much beloved in Texas. Yes, sir. I will tell my children the same. Sir, the reason I'm calling is to ask, as your man in the Southwest, as the owner of the largest newspaper between here and the Pacific Ocean, as someone who has supported you always, if you will kindly do me a personal favor. Yes, sir. I know I don't have to remind you. But this is a big ask. You already gave me a plant. Now I need an extra 30 feet or so. Yes, sir. Let me explain Mr. President. We're Texas, and we want the biggest everything. If Tulsa's is a mile long, mine's gotta be longer. Yes, sir. An extra 30 feet will make me happy. Thank you, Mr. President. I appreciate that, sir. 30 feet. See you soon."

Well, I got my extra footage. Largest bomber plant in the world. Fully automated, the first of its kind. Two million square feet. Air conditioned, too. And like everybody else, we helped win that gosh darn war. It's still there making the greatest fighter jets in the world. Lockheed Martin.

Great news in January 1941.
This almost didn't happen.

—News Staff Photo.

...ined in the rain-filled sky at ground-breaking ceremonies for the Consolidated Aircraft Corpora-...per assembly plant at Fort Worth Friday afternoon is an Army bomber zooming over the speak-...m while Publisher Amon G. Carter (extreme left), master of ceremonies, gazes at the air giant.
United States flags whipped in the rain as the drenched crowd roared at sight of the bomber.

28 Set
Election
...nator

...iel Still Silent
Whether He'll
Office or Not

...of The News.
...Texas, April 18.—Gov.
...Daniel Friday issued a
...n designating Saturday,
...r a special election to
...ited States Senator to
...ainder of the term of
...rris Sheppard, ending
...12. The proclamation
...county judges to take
...y steps to hold the elec-
...y county and election
...Texas.
...law fixing sixty days
...icancy as the earliest
...e election and ninety
...st, the Governor could
...ated June 9 as the
...or July 9 as the latest.
...ay nearly midway be-
...leaving seventy days
...ing.
...ave no hint Friday as
...e will run or whom he
...to serve in the interim
...ection. His five-point
...enate platform given
...d his advocacy of one
...nts, abolition of the
...y, in a personal ap-
...ore the House Friday
...public acts indicating

...udents at the Capitol
...iel might announce in
...adcast Sunday or nos-
...ntil next week, after
...ts on the omnibus tax
...bill carries a sizable
...revenue he is sure to

—News Staff Photo.

Amon G. Carter (right) of Fort Worth and Brig. Gen. G. C. Brant, commander of the Gulf Coast Air Corps Training Center, jointly dug into the site for the new $10,000,000 Consolidated Aircraft Corporation's bomber assembly plant Friday afternoon with a silver spade used in ceremonies.

Coast Air Trainin...
the huddled crow...
ment that a recor...
Air Corps pilot t...
the huge plant v...
ed to Washingto...
Westbrook Wise...
One by one...
stepped from th...
form into the ...
turn at turning...
When Col. 1...
of Washington, ...
ministrator, to...
he grinned:
"I'm the v...
lean on the v...
Prefacing ...
that he was...
Gen. H. H. A...
Corps, Gene...
"Only a f...
Arnold arri...
made a rad...
evening he ...
gave London ...
war. I trust ...
reprisals aft...
"At the o...
land stood ...
France stoo...
Britain and ...
front of the ...
who is back ...
we America...
stand on ou...
Digging Hit...
"We are l...
barked on ...
osition of b...
and trainin...
"This pla...
We're diggi...
Col. Geo...
ington, rep...
partment, ...
was ideal...

See F/...

Pick
Inju
Are

PITTS...
(AP).—T...
cluding ...
dent of t...
nicipal ...
night de...
ing inju...
with a ...
Hospital ...
rested t...
The i...
Frank ...
strained...

Amon broke ground on his bomber plant with Brigadier General G.C. Brant. Amon led so many groundbreakings for businesses he brought to town that his ceremonial shovel collection was unrivaled.

At one mile and nearly 30 feet long, Amon's bomber plant was the longest
in the country and, he bragged, the longest building in the world.

Workers streamed in from
West Texas. The factory
was particularly proud of
its female workers, the
true Rosie the Riveters
of World War II. Here
Mildred Casey, holding
her lunch box, clocked in
for her shift.

Riveters Virginia Foster and Vivian Chlumsky built planes that helped the Allies win World War II.

In this 1945 photo, a worker used a rivet gun on a B-32 "Dominator" bomber at the Consolidated Vultee Aircraft factory.

Thousands of planes have been built in the bomber plant,
now operated by Lockheed Martin.

Mr. Presidents

Folks think I got power. I do in Texas. But it's the president of
the United States who pushes around the big money and the
power to do good.

I make it my business to know my presidents. I write them
letters with suggestions and advice. But mostly I stay on their
good side with truck loads of gifts.

Herbert Hoover gets a smoked turkey every year from me,
even decades after he left the White House.

FDR is my favorite. We got along great. He once visited me
at home. From the back of his touring car, he cast a fishing
line into my pond and yanked out a 5-pound bass.

I knew before most how ill FDR was after I bought him
a new Western belt. Got to keep the old belt as a souvenir.

When you look at the old one, you could see by the notch holes how the president tightened his belt.

He was losing weight under the strain of his long presidency.

Truman and I didn't get along. He vetoed a bill I needed that would allow off-shore oil drilling. Heck, Truman vetoed it twice.

Amon courted the powerful with lavish gifts and attention. But he and President Truman did not get along as famously as Amon did with FDR.

I had a pal, Sid Richardson, an oil man like me. We dabbled in national politics, you could say.

We invited General Eisenhower for a ride of the West-Texan, the *Star-Telegram* yacht kept on Eagle Mountain Lake. Sid and I made the case to Ike to run for president

When Ike announced, I switched from Democrat to Republican for the first time to support him. Ike won, and the new president signed the oil-drilling bill into law.

Trying to help Amon relax, the West Texas Chamber of Commerce bought Amon this 38-foot yacht that he called the West-Texan. In this 1941 photo, he and Junior are at the controls.

According to legend, Amon and fellow oil man Sid Richardson took General Eisenhower on the West-Texan for a private cruise and beseeched him to run for president. Ike did and won. Twice. Here, Amon sits in the stern wearing a captain's hat.

Helping Amon learn to relax was not uncommon in Texas.
In 1939, his business buddies in Fort Worth surprised him
with a gift horse, which they named Will Rogers.

Love of West Texas

A lot of folks who worked at the bomber plant came from
West Texas. They couldn't take the isolation, the hardships
of West Texas any more. Some had to drive a hundred miles
to see a movie or drink a beer.

West Texas needed a champion. West Texas was important.
It produced almost one-half of the world's oil. But the region
was always left behind. Behind the rest of Texas and America
in every significant way: education, medical services, public
utilities, industry, jobs, transportation.

I care about these people. They are my readers. Because
of them, mine was the largest newspaper in Texas for almost
50 years. I care about West Texas because it's Fort Worth's
backyard, the most beautiful backyard a city ever had.

For most of 50 years my newspaper educated, entertained, enlightened, protected, scolded, bragged and gave hope to the good people of West Texas. The newspaper fought for and won roads, universities like Texas Tech, two national parks, including Big Bend, historical monuments and industries. We told farmers about the latest crop prices, gave Mama new recipes, and Junior got his comics and the latest football scores from almost every high school game in the state.

Paper Boy

As the 100th anniversary of the founding of Fort Worth approached in 1949, I drew up plans to go big. I announced to our staff that we were going to produce a commemorative issue that would contain, I hoped, a record number of pages along with the most ad space of any newspaper published in the history of the United States.

We did snare 271 full-page ads; I sold most of them. Everyone wanted to pay tribute to Fort Worth on her beautiful birthday. Or at least they did after I convinced them they did.

I didn't ask. I told.

"I'm putting you down for a full page."

Amon's Full-Page Ad Club.

Amon pulls a copy of the *Star-Telegram* off the new printing press he purchased in 1949. Later that year, he did the same when he wanted early copies of what he bragged was the largest issue of a newspaper ever published.

The Oct. 30, 1949, issue was 480 pages. A world record for a daily newspaper. Heavier than your pet cat.

I was so excited I couldn't sleep. In the middle of the night I yanked a rewrite man off the city desk and ordered a *Star-Telegram* photographer to grab his camera gear. We picked up a fresh bundle of papers, and I started waking up my friends. Pounded on their doors at 4 a.m.

"Wake up! It's Amon Carter. Here's your paper. Don't call me about it not being delivered!"

What fun. And I gotta say, I much admire the pajama styling of the top men of my fair city. As the photos show, they dress up well for the middle of the night.

This sequence of photos proves the story that Amon hand-delivered to his pals, before dawn, copies of the huge *Star-Telegram* issue celebrating Fort Worth's 100th anniversary.

My Wives

I am a lucky man. I married three terrific women. Sympathy to them. Who could put up with me?

My first wife Zetta complained that I "traveled too much" and "sought public esteem and personal adulation."

My second wife Nenetta called me a "marvelous father, the worst husband." She and I formed the Amon G. Carter Foundation at the end of World War II and stayed friends for life. My third wife was Minnie. Our union was the talk of the town. No one could believe it.

Minnie's dad was H.C. Meacham, who owned a department store. He was also Fort Worth's mayor. The city's original airport is named after him.

He and I were best pals, then had the biggest falling out. We were both steel-willed. It lasted till the day he died.

H.C. used to buy 10 pages of ads per week for his store. But he got sore when I didn't endorse him for mayor. He won anyway and swore he'd never buy another ad from me. That cost me $100,000 a year. It cost his store in sales, too.

His name disappeared from my newspaper. I ordered my editors to refer only to Municipal Airport.

Then in 1947, long after the mayor died, I married his daughter Minnie.

You know, that sent tongues a-wagging.

P.S. A few days after H.C. died, his store managers rushed to buy ads in time for Christmas. Sales perked up.

No Tree in '53

The year 1953 was terrible for me. Multiple heart attacks. I missed the dedication ceremony of Amon Carter Field.

That year, we held a city election to approve a new bond. But voters turned it down because they didn't want more taxes.

What about progress? Don't the voters read my editorials? Every year, I send a reporter to New Mexico to bring home the perfect Christmas tree for our city park. My gift to my city.

But after failure at the polls, I'm in no mood. I call the reporter back to the office.

Forget the tree, I tell him. To heck with them.

I wish I hadn't done that.

For Art's Sake

Will Rogers first taught me about art. He said if you like the Wild West, Amon, you'd love the paintings of Frederic Remington and Charles Russell. I bought my first Russell in 1928. Picked up my first Remington in 1935.

From then on, I bought those two whenever their works became available. I purchased entire collections from collectors and galleries.

In 1938, I got took. Bought some Remingtons that turned out to be fakes. After that, I needed letters of authenticity.

With more than 200 paintings and bronze statues as a start, my daughter Ruth was able to lead the construction of the Amon Carter Museum of American Art, which opened in 1961.

Ask the experts. It's considered one of the finest museums in the world.

Best part: As per instructions in my will, admission is always free.

The Amon Carter Museum of American Art is considered one of the nation's finest showcases for Americana. The museum opened fewer than six years after his death.

Under Ruth Carter Stevenson, her father's dream of a world-class museum quickly took shape; in the process, she became one of America's leading art experts. Here, she posed with Winslow Homer's *Crossing the Meadow*.

My 50-Year Run

I RUN A NEWSPAPER, but as you can see, I run the town, too. Politicians come to me for support. If I like 'em, they get endorsed with lots of coverage. If I don't, their names may hardly appear.

Is that fair? Probably not, but that worked for a long, long time. Then this Jim Wright kid comes along and, well, he got in my face.

My guy, Congressman Wingate Lucas, was running for a new term. His opponent was this young man, the mayor of Weatherford, Wright. In our coverage, we ignore the kid. He speaks at a rally before a thousand people, but we don't mention it.

After we endorse Wingate, the kid is furious. He pays $974 for a full-page ad in my newspaper. No one ever bought an ad like this before.

"OPEN LETTER TO MR. AMON G. CARTER," the ad announced.

"You have at last met a man, Mr. Carter, who is not afraid of you...who will not bow his knee to you...and come running like a simpering pup at your beck and call."

Wright called Wingate my "private errand-boy congressman" and declared, "The people are tired of 'One-Man-Rule.' This is a new day. New blood and new minds and new thoughts, fresh from the people themselves, are needed.... It is unhealthy for ANYONE to become too powerful."

It works. This Wright kid wins the congressional seat.

Long after I'm gone, Congressman Wright is elected Speaker of the U.S. House of Representatives.

Not bad for a kid from my West Texas.

Died on Deadline

I died the boss. 1955. I'm not gonna use my time machine to go there. Once was enough.

But it was a warm night in June. I was a newspaperman to the end. I died 40 minutes before deadline. Time to make it into the paper that hits the doorsteps of all my friends across West Texas. My obituary:

Amon G. Carter Sr. died at 8:20 p.m. Thursday. Death came to the publisher at his home. Carter had been in ill health since 1953 when he suffered two heart attacks.

Aw, I can't read any more of this. Yeah, some things even I can't fix.

My friend J.C. Penney said: "Fort Worth is not where the West begins. The West is wherever Amon Carter is."

After I left, they shuffled through my private papers and saw all the things I did quietly. Ruth Carter Stevenson, my Sugar Pie, built the Carter museum. A grand city needs a grand museum. Ruth became one of the nation's top experts on American art.

I used the oil money to start the Amon G. Carter Foundation. Oh, I had to do that. My wife Nenetta and I had prayed during World War II: "If God will give us back our son, we will spend the rest of our lives trying to help others."

And all these years later, the foundation we started has given out more than $600 million. And Junior? He successfully ran the empire for another 20-plus years. So proud of my kids.

Good Deeds

I'd hear about a TCU student who couldn't afford a train ticket home to see his family—and buy him a ticket. Somebody in a terrible automobile wreck? Might pay their hospital bill. House burned down? You get the idea.

People never knew who the MYSTERIOUS BENEFACTOR was. Made me feel good to be able to do that. Especially when I bought the old boarding house in Bowie where I worked as a boy. Gave it to the landlady, Mrs. Jarrott. Paid all her expenses, paid for her funeral, too. Made me feel good.

To this day, Bowie hosts a yearly "Chicken and Bread Days Heritage Festival." No fooling!

Sure my name is around, but most modern folks, I'm sure they're swell, they don't remember me. I led the first board of Texas Tech. You've got Amon Carter Riverside High. Amon Carter Boulevard. Camp Carter. Amon Carter BloodCare. Amon Carter Stadium. There's a Lake Amon G. Carter. Oh, and there's even an Amon Carter Peak in Big Bend. How 'bout that? My own little mountaintop. They say the view from up there is, like me, unforgettable.

I'm pretty lucky. First, they named an airport hanger after me, then a whole terminal. And for a while, an airport was named after me, too. How 'bout that?"

I built a city. Lured a trillion dollars' worth of business. Yep, I taught my employees the cardinal rule: *You can't live off your community. You must live with it.*

I hope it always stays that way for newspapers.

Amon Carter Riverside High School in Fort Worth.

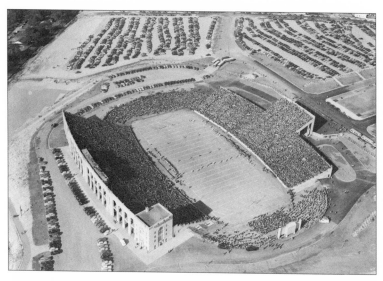

Amon Carter Stadium at Texas Christian University. Amon never attended college, or even high school, yet he adopted TCU as if it were his own.

As a young teen, Amon worked at Millie Jarrott's boarding house in Bowie. In exchange for room and board, he was janitor, handyman and chambermaid. He never forgot his roots. He paid bills for Jarrott the rest of her life, then funded her funeral.

Finale

WHEN WE STARTED THIS, we were strangers but now we're friends! Don't forget you're a member of Amon's Full-Page Advertising Club. I'll leave you with these thoughts.

- In order to understand the future, you must know the past. Don't ever forget.
- We each have the opportunity to make a difference in our cities and in the lives of others, and it's not all about money. It's about giving. Giving our time. Giving our respect.
- *"A man cannot live off his community. He must live with it."*

Okay, lesson's over. Remember that our beloved Fort Worth is where the West begins. God bless Texas. And may God bless you.

Henry David Thoreau once said, "Live your life, do your work, then take your hat."

Amon Through the Years

Amon Carter in 1882, age 3.

A series taken in 1897 when Amon would have been about 18 years old.

Amon in an undated photo,
probably in the 1890s.

Amon, probably taken in 1927.

Playing cowboy for his annual Christmas Day portrait. This one is in 1944.

Undated photo.

In 1939, the Fort Worth Club, which Amon served as president for decades, honored him with this portrait.

Acknowledgments

THE SOMEWHAT FORGOTTEN STORY of Amon G. Carter's oversized influence came alive for me 20 years ago after reading the terrific biography by my former *Star-Telegram* colleague, the late Jerry Flemmons.

His book, *Amon: The Texan Who Played Cowboy for America*, is one of the finest journalism biographies I've read. Everything about Fort Worth—from its physical layout to its industries and deep commitment to community—suddenly made sense to me. What a revelation.

For this book and the play of the same name, I found primary source materials—Amon's own words in many cases—to help me tell these stories. Hundreds upon hundreds of boxes of his papers and photographs are stored at Texas Christian University, where the Mary Couts Burnett Library is ably led by Mary Saffell. Carter curator Allison Kirchner knows much about Amon. And Lisa Pena shepherded me through the hundreds of boxes of Amon's papers and photographs.

The University of Texas at Arlington Libraries' Special Collections is led by Brenda McClurkin with assistance by Sara Pezzoni, caretakers of the vast, archival collection of

Fort Worth Star-Telegram photos. They also provided photos from other collections in their care—the W.D. Smith Commercial Photography Collection, the Jack White Photograph Collection and the Squire Haskins Photography Collection.

Bomber plant photos are courtesy of Lockheed Martin, Ken Ross and the University of North Texas Digital Library.

Thanks to archivists at the Herbert Hoover Presidential Library in Iowa, who put up with my unscheduled pop-in while I was in town for a speech.

I enjoyed the doctoral dissertation *Lone Star Booster: The Life of Amon G. Carter* by Texas history professor Brian Cervantez, which led to his 2019 book, *Amon Carter: A Lone Star Life,* published by University of Oklahoma Press. Cervantez attempts to place Carter in the historical perspective of his time and place, as a leader in the Southwest. His scholarly work emphasizes the cultural forces that shaped Carter and how Carter shaped his community.

I learned about Broadway Billy Rose from Mark Cohen's fun new book, *Not Bad for Delancey Street: The Rise of Billy Rose.*

Anita Robeson, my longtime book editor, super-proofed this manuscript under tight deadlines so we could publish before the world premiere of the play at Artisan Center Theater in Hurst, Texas, on May 9, 2019.

Watching a group of experts like the crew at ACT take my words on a page and turn them into art on stage is a sight every writer should experience once in a lifetime.

I am proud of my association with Artisan, one of the largest community theaters in Texas. I first wrote about Artisan in its opening year, 15 years ago, in my *Star-Telegram* column. Back again, this time as a playwright, we've come full circle together. Artisan is everything you could hope for in a neighborhood community theater—and much, much more—as evident of the inherent risk of producing a new play by a first-time playwright.

At Artisan, I thank for their hard work on this new play: DeeAnn Blair (founder and executive producer); Richard Blair (founder, executive producer); Dorothy Sanders (founder); Natalie Burkhart (associate producer); Eric Luckie (scene designer, set construction); Amy Luckie (prop mistress, archivist); Oliver Lukach (scenic shop supervisor); Jeff Watson (scenic designer, historian, set construction); Doug Vandegrift (scenic design, illuminations); Brian Blair (graphic designer); Connie Sanchez (director, costume designer, set conceptualization and design); Kelvin Dilks (principal actor), and Joe Allen Brown, Texas Wesleyan University professor, (consultant, Artistic, Thematic and Technical Advisor).

I have the best book designers in Texas with Austin's TLC Book Design, led by Tamara Dever and Monica Thomas. We'll celebrate this book's release at a Billy Joel concert.

Thanks to photographer Renee Strayley for the author photo and Norm Sunshine for making arrangements.

Thanks to Jon Perry and Vanessa Lang for keeping the business and design portion of the DaveLieber.org website ticking properly.

At *The Dallas Morning News*, thanks to my editor, Dave Hiott, who was a terrific sounding board as I tested various concepts related to this project in between planning each week's double dose of "The Watchdog" investigative column.

At the *Fort Worth Star-Telegram*, thanks to the long-ago editors who made the risky decision to bring me to Texas more than 25 years ago to launch a Lieber metro column—Mike Blackman, Bruce Raben and then-publisher Rich Connor. Thanks to publisher Wes Turner for keeping me.

I appreciate the help from family and friends who read the play script and saw greater possibilities than I did. Thanks to brother Bennett Lieber and sister-in-law Nancy Distel; Kelly and Scott Bradley; storytelling master Doug Stevenson; sidekick Marina Trahan Martinez; My Computer Guy Scott Green; TV pro David Duitch; and marketing wizard Homer Plankton. Steve Kaplan was an early theater/drama/comedy influence when I was a teen, and I'm glad we reconnected after 45 years.

Thanks to Jamie Knight for creating the play's official website, AmonPlay.com. And thanks to Tyler Cox, the former Operations/Program manager at WBAP, for his excellent work recording the audiobook of *AMON! The Ultimate Texan*.

John Dycus helped me set up a preview of portions of the play at a December 2018 gathering of the Society of Professional Journalists/Fort Worth chapter, which I expanded into a reunion for *Star-Telegram* alumni. Thanks to all who attended that fun night.

My friends at First Christian Church in Arlington were the first audience upon which I tested a few scenes of the play. When it comes to unveiling my newest project, that church is my good-luck charm.

Mark Haney, one of Texas' top lawyers, lent me rights to use the song *Fort Worth Texas*.

When I couldn't find an Amon Carter family tree, genealogist Denise Maine put one together for me.

Jeff Prince of *Fort Worth Weekly* and Karen Gavis of the *Dallas Observer* were the first reporters to bring attention to the companion play.

My writing pals at the National Society of Newspaper Columnists are always supportive of my we-can-do-this ideas.

My speaking pals at the National Speakers Association are magical influences in my life, helping me keep my creativity at full throttle. I'd love to name them all here, but there are hundreds. Special people.

Huge shout-out to my emotional support gang, my backbone, the Fab 5, Sally Baskey, Christine Cashen, Tim Durkin and Michael Hoffman, and their spouses, Gary, Gregg, Julie and Michele.

Extra special thanks to DeeAnn and Rick Blair of Artisan Center Theater who latched onto this project on New Year's Day 2019 and, along with his crew, brought it to the stage a mere four months later.

Finally, most important, my wife, Karen, worked as a true partner on this project, as she always does in everything. She helped me get this done despite a grueling newspaper schedule that often had me working 80 hours a week. How did I write this? On our rare vacations.

I know.

I owe her a real one.

~DAVE LIEBER

About the Author

DAVE LIEBER has worked as a national-award-winning newspaperman for more than 40 years, the last 26 as the butt-kicking "Watchdog" columnist for the *Fort Worth Star-Telegram* and then *The Dallas Morning News*.

He received his training as a young reporter at *The Philadelphia Inquirer* during its glory days of the 1980s.

Dave has written eight books. He's also a certified professional speaker (one of only a thousand in the world) who entertains audiences—and also teaches businesses, groups and individuals how to use strategic storytelling to attract followers and lead change.

For more on this, watch his popular TED Talk, "The Power of Storytelling to Change the World," at DaveLieber.org.

Dave's theater background is slight. As a pre-pubescent youth, he sang boy soprano in the children's chorus at the Metropolitan Opera. As a teen, he co-hosted with other teens a live, unscripted national TV show Saturday mornings on NBC called *Take a Giant Step*. Young Dave also studied at the famed Stella Adler Studio of Acting in Manhattan. After that, nothing. Journalism called.

In 1994, Dave proposed to his wife in his newspaper column ("Here, in Texas, I've met the woman of my dreams. Unfortunately, she lives with the dog of my nightmares.") Karen and Dave have three children, Desiree, Jonathan and Austin.

Dave is a member of the Dramatists Guild of America.

AMON! The Ultimate Texan is his first play.

Dave Lieber

CERTIFIED PROFESSIONAL SPEAKER

W HEN AMON CARTER was around, he held the micro-phone. He *always* held the microphone.

He was the master of ceremonies, always the emcee.

Center stage was his space and no one else's.

But Amon is long gone.

Now it's Dave Lieber who holds the microphone, who serves as a favored emcee, who, as one of America's top storytelling experts, teaches businesses, groups and individuals how to replace boring facts and figures with emotional, unforgettable stories.

Dave has spoken to more than 1,800 audiences in Texas, the U.S., Mexico and Canada. He's a certified professional speaker through the National Speakers Association. There are only a thousand presenters in the world who've earned that designation.

Now that Amon is gone, Dave Lieber is one of Texas' most popular speakers. Bring Dave to your group for fun, laughter and learning.

~FOR MORE INFORMATION~
Visit: DaveLieber.org
Call: (800) 557-8166
Write: Speaker@YankeeCowboy.com

Y'all come back now!

AmonPlay.com